P·R·A·Y·E·R·S
from a Nonbeliever

◆

◆

Plays

Public Lives
The Animal in the Trees
Four Roses
Love in the DMZ
Avalon (A MUSICAL)
Bloodlines
The Medium at Large (A MUSICAL)
Tinseltown (A MUSICAL)
Normal, Nebraska (A MUSICAL)

◆

Poetry

Prayers for the Little Ones
Prayers for the Nature Spirits
The Quiet Animal
The Earth (ALSO AN ALBUM WITH TIM WHEATER)

◆

Feature Film
(AS WRITER-DIRECTOR)

God's Will

JEREMY P. TARCHER • PUTNAM

A MEMBER OF

PENGUIN PUTNAM INC.

NEW YORK

P·R·A·Y·E·R·S
from a Nonbeliever

· *A Story of Faith* ·

Julia Cameron

Most Tarcher/Putnam books are available at special quantity discounts
for bulk purchase for sales promotions, premiums, fund-raising, and
educational needs. Special books or book excerpts also can be created
to fit specific needs. For details, write Putnam Special Markets,
375 Hudson Street, New York, NY 10014.

Jeremy P. Tarcher/Putnam
a member of
Penguin Putnam Inc.
375 Hudson Street
New York, NY 10014
www.penguinputnam.com

Library of Congress Cataloging-in-Publication Data

Cameron, Julia.
Prayers from a nonbeliever : a story of faith / Julia Cameron.
p.   cm.
ISBN 1-58542-213-4 (alk. paper)
1. Spiritual life—Miscellanea.   I. Title.
BL624.C33192   2003   2002034770
291.4'33—dc21

Printed in the United States of America
3   5   7   9   10   8   6   4   2

This book is printed on acid-free paper. ∞

BOOK DESIGN BY DEBORAH KERNER/DANCING BEARS DESIGN

To H.O.F.

with love and gratitude

◆

PRAYERS
from a Nonbeliever

◆

Dear God,

I do not have an easy relationship to you, God. I am confused by your press. I have read so much about you, from so many quarrelsome experts, that I do not know who you are—*if* you are. And yet, I suppose you are—something made all this—and so I thought I would try to make contact.

I doubt that I will do this right. I do not know how to do this right. But I think the fact that I am trying should count for something.

Where should I begin? I like your world. With all its flaws and suffering, it is still beautiful. Perhaps we agree on that. Who knows? Maybe we agree on my gripe about "God Experts," too. They make it feel so hard to know you.

Yesterday, I lay down on a patch of grass and pressed my head to the earth as if I could hear your heart. Maybe I did. Today I wrote you this first prayer.

Dear God,

As I mentioned, I am trying to "just show up" and see what happens in relationship to you. I have been carrying my agnostic banner for a long time, and then I got the uncomfortable idea that maybe I wasn't so much agnostic as lazy. I hadn't drawn a dignified conclusion of nonbelief. I just couldn't be bothered to do the research. So I am experimenting with you—hey, it's only fair. We—this world—are your experiment, aren't we? Do you have a sense of humor?

Maybe you do. Baboons with their fire-engine asses are pretty funny. Also anteaters. Sloths. Tarantulas, if I weren't afraid of them. And perhaps me. I'm funny too: a middle-age person belatedly thinking, *Gee, maybe I'd better try doing something around this God thing.*

The truth is, you are confusing. It seems to me

that making a violet would take a certain amount of care and attention, even tenderness. But at night, that vast swathe of stars spewed across all that black—what does that take? Perhaps a grandiose indifference? Maybe the coldness that numbers seem to imply. But maybe not to you.

It occurs to me that in trying to know you, explore your mind—if you can be said to have such a thing—I may actually get to know my own. That, perhaps, is not such a bad thing.

Dear God,

Full disclosure: I am only undertaking these prayers as an experiment at the suggestion of a friend. I have not had any spiritual awakening, and I frankly doubt that I ever will. My friend, who is a bit perky and even New Age, if you ask me, suggested I try thinking of you as "an invisible playmate." In light of things like death and the Holocaust, that made me feel like I was trying to talk to the Invisible Bully. Will I get struck by lightning for saying that?

As I have said from the beginning, I don't officially believe in you—although even logic seems to say something must have made all this. It's funny how I can not believe in you and still blame you. I guess I think of you a bit like God the Father after all—you know how kids always blame their parents.

But I do not think I want a parent-child relationship with you. I am not sure I want any relationship at all, but I do wonder if I might not be late to the party. Maybe we've already got a relationship and I am just pretending we don't. Kind of like, "Alright, I put my arm around you at the movie, but it didn't mean anything, so don't get carried away."

Don't get carried away, God. These letters don't mean I am your new best friend. I am just thinking about you. If there is a you, that is. Funny how just entertaining that possibility makes it seem somehow more *possible*. Do you think prayer is the greased slide to faith?

Dear God,

What follows is the kind of prayer you don't want to get. I'd call it whining and it certainly shouldn't get priority over prayers for starving children, world peace, or any other noble cause that crosses your venue.

As you know—since you are God, after all—I am talking about my life: my cushy, privileged, nicer-than-most life. I have almost exactly the life I always said I wanted, and I don't really like it very much. My creature comforts are adequate—more than adequate. I could use the same word for my friends. Then, too, there's the arena of professional accomplishment, in which I am, well, accomplished. The point is that my life is stuffed to the gills with people, places, and things that ought to make me happy but don't. So I feel like an ingrate. Or a cliché.

Is this what they mean by "midlife crisis"? I have heard the phrase "dark night of the soul" bandied about, but that seems a little melodramatic for what is essentially the old Peggy Lee complaint: "If that's all there is . . ."

You can see why I feel like I am whining. I *am* whining. It's not so much that there's something wrong with your world—check out the sunset last night, for example. It's my world, my "inner world," that's off-kilter.

My friends are full of advice, ranging from the ridiculous to the ridiculous and all of it probably good or good enough—we're a reasonably enlightened crowd. I have been told to get a hobby. A new relationship. An advanced degree. A Jungian therapist. A puppy. A service commitment to some worthy cause. Maybe I will do all that stuff—alright, even like it—but it all seems a little topiary, like I am shaping the edges of my life and not addressing the problem—the void—at the center.

That's why you're hearing from me. Better late than never.

If you have any thoughts, you know my e-mail. Actually, how do you answer prayers?

Dear God,

My friends have begun to back off. Let's face it: A dark night of the soul is not a social asset. When I tell them what I'm thinking about, namely you, the existence or the nonexistence of you, they make worried little sounds as if I'm having a breakdown. Nonetheless, they're full of good advice. As I've told you, hobbies, therapists, kittens, a renewed love life—all these things are mentioned as the cure. When I say they sound more like distractions, I'm treated like I've gone too far. My friends take it personally when I reject their advice. The word they use among themselves is "crackpot," as in, "He's got some crackpot idea about getting to know God." Is this a crackpot idea? Perhaps you could talk to my friends.

Dear God,

I have an ulterior motive with these prayers. I am hoping to attain something of an overview, a broader perspective. I am not talking about "child dies, leaf falls from tree—same value." But I am thinking that if I could attain what is probably called faith, I might have an easier time of things, a sneaking optimism, a suspicion that just maybe everything will work out after all.

Living in a city makes that harder, I think. There's the everyday crush, of course, but there's also the fact that cities seem to be about what man has made, and the rest of creation gets marginalized. I mean, an Omaha farmer watches a field go cold and dead and gray. Omaha in winter is a hellish place, but then spring! Little green shoots. Bigger green shoots. Corn. Pardon the pun, God, but something as corny as corn can make you trust that

life has more up its sleeve than the apparent win-
try disaster of the moment. I mean, there must be a
balance—at least as much beauty and hope in this
world as disaster—but we don't focus on that. The
evening news is not good. But it's not the whole
story, either. My thought is that maybe you hold a
larger view than CNN. That's why I am trying to
tune in to you instead.

Is there a you?

Dear God,

My sister is a good woman. As you may have noticed, she goes to church every week, and she's kind to her neighbors. She also does a considerable amount of work with the Animal Rescue League, and she's always taking in strays to nurse back to health. They flourish under her care. I wish she'd turn the same attention to herself. She wouldn't give a pet to a bad home. Why doesn't she see that *she* deserves a good one? Personally, I think her ne'er-do-well husband wants a mommy, not a wife, and then maybe a few girlfriends on the side, to which he mysteriously feels entitled. Was I standing behind the door when the entitlement gene was passed out? Was my sister? I guess my simple point is this: I'm at my wit's end. I've listened to my sister's woes with as much patience as I can muster. I'm about to do something rash. How do you stand it, listening to us all? And do we ever do what you think we should?

Dear God,

I am uncomfortable with what has been happening to me since I started writing to you. I would even blame you—if I believed in you. I seem to be looking at my life with different eyes—seeing where I have settled, where I have said, "This is probably as good as it gets," even when that wasn't good enough. I see that I have not stepped up to the plate in a lot of areas. I have just said, "What's the use? It probably wouldn't work out anyhow."

"It probably wouldn't work out" has dissuaded me from a lot of risks—risks that if I thought there were a you, a supportive you, I might have tried taking. I am beginning to get the uncomfortable feeling that my world is too small and that I can try, comfortably, to blame that on you—but I might be the real culprit.

I'd like a new place to live—something larger,

brighter, and still affordable. I've told myself I probably can't find it, so I am not even looking. That lets both me and you off the hook. Neither of us has to lift a finger to improve my life. The problem is, I am now wondering, *If I lifted my finger, would you lift yours?* Why do I think the answer is yes?

Dear God,

I do not like having my life shaken up—even if that's what I've been asking for. I was pretty comfortable in my misery—even if I was miserable. I had a routine and I stuck to it. I didn't like it and I blamed it on you—or the lack of you.

Now I have a routine that I don't like, and I am starting to blame it on me—or the lack of me. In other words, a lot of what I thought of as your shortfall may have been my own.

This all goes back a long way. God dumped me on Earth into a poor family so I couldn't fully develop my confidence and my gifts. That's what I have tried to tell myself, and I have held a grudge about it, believe me. Now I think—ever since starting to write you these damn letters—maybe I got placed in that family on purpose, precisely so I could develop my confidence and my gifts by my own hand.

I feel like I am having figure-ground reversal. Do you know what I mean? (Of course *you* do.) It's when you look at a drawing one way and it's a vase, and then you look again and it's two women's faces. Both are equally possible and perhaps equally true—all depending on how you look at it. As an agnostic, I comfortably looked at it in the negative way. Now—and I would not say I am a believer—as an experimenter with this God business, I am suddenly seeing another and more positive possibility. My life looks less like wreckage and more like building materials. Is that why they call you the Creator?

Dear God,

You probably will not find this reasonable, but it has always seemed reasonable to me to act as if you do not exist. In other words, instead of waiting for you to come along and save the day, I do something about things myself. Maybe this is the real reason churches and synagogues get involved with the poor, with soup kitchens, and with homeless shelters. They don't trust you, either. The starving? Well, try to feed them. The homeless? Try to shelter them. The problem with this self-sufficiency, of course, is that it relies a lot on my rather limited resources and reserves of time, energy, money, and for that matter, goodwill.

I think what I was doing was actually rather dualistic. I tried to have it both ways. I could point to the world's problems and say either there was no God or else there was a lousy one. I could point to the good I was doing and feel like God myself until I just got exhausted—or simply human—and then I felt there must be something more, but I was too stubborn to ask for help and maybe, if I admit it, afraid that if I tried to find you I would not be able to. Maybe a little like a child scared in his room, not crying for help in case the house really is empty.

Dear God,

I would like to know your opinion of Santa Claus and whether or not you feel—as I do—that people seem to get you and Santa confused. I know a lot of people who talk about prayer like it's their Christmas wish list. They seem to spend their time badgering you for toys. That always seemed beneath your dignity and mine.

On the other hand, maybe I act like the orphan who is too proud to ask for any help at all. Maybe I don't want to hear "no," so I just don't ask. Maybe I need some way to think about you that is not so anthropomorphic—you with a long beard and twinkly eyes, or you with a stony face, furled brow, and a Michelangelo finger pointing me straight to hell.

This is where ideas like "The Force" and the Tao and words like Spirit and even Universe might be useful—although they do seem to me to be mincing words. Aren't we really talking about God, after all? But I like the idea of thinking of you as some form of spiritual electricity, the life force, intelligent, outreaching, meticulous, intricate. To me there is beauty in that and maybe some accuracy if I don't make it cold and mechanistic.

Do you care if we believe in you or what we believe you to be? Do you even—and here's a scary thought—respond to us in terms of our beliefs? Those who need a Santa Claus God get Santa Claus; those who need fancy existential doubts get what they ask for.

In other words, maybe believing in you, even badly or wrongly or naively, throws some kind of spiritual circuit breaker, and the "juice" of support starts to flow.

It's possible.

Dear God,

Or the way I am feeling today: "Dear God!" You are apprised, I suppose, of yesterday's horrific news. Another bloodbath in the name of religious differences. The cradle of civilization—as we once called the Middle East—is a powder keg again, and the news is full of images you may be all too familiar with: mutilated bodies, weeping mothers, stricken survivors stumbling through the streets. After I watch the news, I stumble through the streets. It is all so terrible.

"Not *all*," I can almost hear you saying. "There is beauty everywhere." Maybe from your altitude, but not from mine. From mine it looks like another bloody century is kicking off as has many a bloody century before it. You may have the higher view, but living here—and having CNN—I have the inside skinny.

How can you let that sort of thing go on? Or maybe the question is: How can I? I have been told, "God speaks through other people," but if that's so, I feel like a lot of what you say is like Tourette's syndrome, a curse upon us all.

Some say that these feelings of despair are just a little trick you use to get us talking to you.

Well, fine, the trick worked. But I resent it. I resent it more than you can imagine, but there is probably nothing you can't imagine—including the redemption of our miserable lot.

How can you be an optimist after all this time— and all this carnage?

Dear God,

Now we really have something to talk about. I'm talking about 9/11, of course. All those innocent people. How could you?

I suppose you saw the images. Horrific. Even on cloud nine, you couldn't miss them. The networks and CNN broadcast nothing but. Do I need to remind you that this atrocity was committed in your name? The terrorists thought they were doing something good? To me, it seemed unspeakably evil, the more so when they published the list of airline passengers and I saw an old friend's name on the scroll. She was a lovely woman, believe me, with two lovely children. I certainly hope you're enjoying her company, because they certainly miss her. Thanks for nothing. Where were you when we needed you?

Dear God,

These letters are a habit. I'm not speaking to you, but I'm writing to you. I've heard your excuses about 9/11. You didn't do it, we did. You simply allowed it. How do you reconcile that with the "Our Father," the prayer Jesus taught? What kind of father would just stand there and watch one child murder another? Did I hear you say "free will"?

Dear God,

Maybe it takes a good emergency to bring people to their senses. Maybe that's the purpose—the silver lining, if there is one. There are collections for the firefighters' families; money and clothes are welcome. I learned on the news that shrines are appearing on the streets of Manhattan, that people are invoking God's mercy for the victims and their families. Well, it's the least you could do. I donated cash and some khakis that never fit right. One of those shrines cropped up outside my building. It was a bookcase with some candles on its shelves and the smiling framed faces of some men who are now dead. Oh, yes, a cross topped it off. I guess that was the address, so you'd notice. The talk shows say that a renewed faith in God is one of the results of the tragedy. That should please you. Pardon my sarcasm (from the Greek, "to cut or tear flesh"). I guess this anger of mine is getting tiresome. I guess that what really bothers me isn't what you did, but what we did.

Dear God,

I am experiencing a heightened and uncomfortable restlessness, which, it has occurred to me, might be normal and even intentional on your part. I'd like to take something apart or put something together. "Creative energy," I guess it's called. Is this how you felt when you made the world?

This morning, walking by the park, I encountered a retired engineer who struck up a conversation. "I'm happily married and thinking about having an affair," he started off. In light of my own experience, I wasn't buying. "That's just creative energy," I told him. "You need a project, not an affair."

"That's too much work." He groaned.

Is this how sin originated? Were we too lazy or too passive to use our energies along creative lines and so we just got into mischief? I think I might be onto something here.

Take pride. The engineer said he was too old to be a beginner again at something. He taught part-time and he enjoyed it because he looked the part of older and wiser, and people actually listened to him.

Well, I listened to him, too. And what I heard wasn't older and wiser.

"I'm going to die soon," he said. "I'm sixty-seven."

"You might have twenty more years," I snapped. "That's plenty of time to do something."

I told him about my friend John who set up a television network in Indochina the year he turned eighty.

So the engineer babbled on, overflowing with both ideas and excuses and I—perhaps because I have been writing to you—found myself thinking, *Mmm. God must see this kind of thing all the time.* We must constantly seem like underachievers. You certainly had the humility to start over and over as a beginner: daffodil, dahlia, daisy, dandelion—and that's just the D's.

Well, God, this is what I was thinking about you. Are you really thinking about me?

Dear God,

My skepticism is exhausting me. I act like I am a titan heaving the modern world on his shoulders. God forbid—although you haven't—I ask for any help. I want to pass it off as an instinct not to bother you, but it may be something closer to "Me Do It Self"—evidently, my first words as a toddler. Take my job (yes, take it!). I hate my boss, I resent my balky coworkers, and what I do about all of it is over-work, harboring a grudge. Is that babyish enough for you?

Theologically, it feels as if I am still in diapers. I stubbornly insist on my independence and then I get overwhelmed—like a two-year-old who wants to walk alone, makes it across the living room, and then collapses. It is only in the collapses that I recognize my essential arrogance.

Dear God,

Well, I tried. I suppose you're going to tell me I caught him on an off day. But church just isn't for me. I should have known better than to risk a "God Expert." Can't you see how unattractive your system is? They make you out to be something like the Wizard of Oz, a grand poobah behind the screen, accessible only through lackeys and toadies. Couldn't you come up with something better? Certainly paganism has more appeal. Dancing under the open skies in some grove, copulating in the name of God—a little strenuous, perhaps, but certainly more cheerful. My point is, I don't know how to approach you like a curriculum. "God as told to me by . . ." I do a little better stumbling along, trying to know you or at least let you know me through these clumsy prayers.

Dear God,

I would not dignify this passage of my life by calling it "the dark night of the soul," but it is dark—or at least murky. It's a little foreboding, like one of those fog shots in a horror movie, the swirling mists right before the zombie steps out of the swamp. It may not look that way to you. For you, this may be a minor overcast as you watch the bright weather over Kansas moving toward me. I do not have the benefit of your higher perspective. To me, my life is more like a maze—clear enough to you up above, but down here it's all walking into walls and stumbling through switchbacks and reverses.

"Stop writing," I thought I just heard you say. "Stick to the facts." OK. Fact: I am pretty goddamn confused. Pardon the language. I am restless, irritable, cross, wonderful to live with I am sure, and there is nothing officially wrong.

Tragedy I can deal with. I don't like to, but I can. When a parent dies, you know it is a big thing, and even I know enough to be patient and gentle with myself. But this? This malcontent doesn't inspire any inward compassion. This is more the inspiration for self-flagellation and anger. I try to reason with myself, which basically means scold myself. It goes like this: *Oh, for Christ's sake* (there I go again) *get a grip. Your life is fine. You've got more than a lot of people. More than you ever thought you'd have. Certainly more than your sister's got. Now you're just a whining spoilsport. You want something "more," but you don't even know what that is.*

God, do you know what that something more is? Could you tell me? And if you are trying to talk to me, how will I know it? What do I do to hear you? You could try Priority Mail.

Dear God,

My boss's father has Alzheimer's. I learned this from his secretary. He was in one of his usual moods, maybe a little worse, and she tried to explain. It seems the boss visits him every Saturday, but there's no recognition. Or he calls him by his brother's name. I can't quite picture him as the dutiful son, but evidently he is one. And maybe I should cut him a break.

Which brings me to another idea: Is it really true that you love us all equally? How could you? I have heard you called "Mother, Father God," but could any parent really think of Hitler as their naughty little boy? All right, my boss is not Hitler, even though we call him that behind his back. But he's not lovable, or if he is, it's to you and his wife. Maybe you gave the family Alzheimer's just to even things out. One of the worst things he does is call employees by the wrong names. Maybe now he'll know how it feels. Am I petty? I suppose so. Well, I'm told you will love me anyway. Just testing the waters, I guess.

Dear God,

My left foot has a nasty blister, thank you very much.

I am blaming you because, after yesterday's letter, I got the idea—inspiration?—that I might be able to hear you more clearly if I went on a few walks. So I went on a great big walk. And my shoe pinched. And I ignored it. And now I have a blister, the large puffy kind, and the very clear idea—inspiration?—that walks are still a good idea.

Not that I myself really got a good idea, you understand. I did not feel you sitting on my shoulder, singing "Zippity Do-Dah" or even "Ave Maria." (If you take requests, what I'd really like is Paul Robeson doing "Amazing Grace.") No, that did not happen. Nothing seemed to happen, but I do notice a certain creeping optimism and humor despite the goddamn (whoops) blister.

You know the phrase—you must—"God is in

the details?" Well, maybe you are in the details. It was the details on the walk that cheered me up. Right on my own block, I noticed a beautiful cornice on the old building with the bad newsstand. The newsstand is still awful and the guy who runs it *really* needs a spiritual awakening, but this cornice—some architect's "inspiration," to give you credit—was a graceful and flowing thing, an ornament like a musical trill, and I have never seen it before.

After that, at the entrance to the park, I noticed a bird's nest—pretty elaborate, almost a high-rise—cantilevered in one of the trees. I saw a *huge* squirrel, and it switched its tail at me like some cartoon squirrel saying, "Cute, aren't I?" Then—and this does sound like a flora and fauna report—I actually spotted a blue heron standing on one leg in that little tiny pond they excavated for Sunday rowing in those dumb little yellow kiddie boats. Also, it occurred to me that my boss was actually worrying about his father's Alzheimer's and not trying to be a bastard. Of course, he still was a bastard (I guess you were, too, if I am talking to Jesus), but the thing is, I felt compassion or at least empathy. And so, I was a little nicer at work today—after I got a Scholl's pad for the goddamn blister.

"Walk with me." Did Jesus say that to his disciples? Or was it in some bad movie? Maybe they all say that. "Walk with me." Gandhi to the sea, Jesus in Jerusalem, Buddha across miles of earth where they happened to have cobras.

Walk with you. I am going to keep trying that.

Dear God,

What is it about family? My sister is having a hard time, and I want to wave a magic wand and play God and fix it. Her louse of a husband has walked out and I am glad, but I just want to hunt him down and kill him—a very spiritual agenda. I am beginning to have respect for your restraint. We must do things that drive you crazy all the time.

Did you say, "Try the Gulf War?" No, you couldn't have. Are my politics showing?

Dear God,

I am in the middle of a transition—there! Now I have found a graceful word for this passage in my life! And I am told by friends and family that I am supposed to "have a little faith." That may mean patience. That may mean optimism despite the perceived odds. That may mean flipping Murphy's Law like a pancake and believing that my life will not land jam-side down. You know Murphy's Law. It's right up there with the Ten Commandments: If you drop a piece of toast, it will always land jam-side down.

In this transition, during which I am supposed to have faith, I am wondering: faith in what? In you? If I start entertaining the notion that you're involved in the pickle I'm in, well, then I will not so much have faith as a whopping resentment.

Have you heard the spiritual bromide, "Nothing happens in God's world by accident?" In light of things like the Gulf War and mudslides in Peru, this makes you out to play real hardball, doesn't it? I think it may be intended to help us weather catastrophe by searching for the silver lining. But if the silver lining is lying in some city street covered by the rubble of a bombed building—decimated in your name, I might add—well, then I would prefer to think some things in your world do happen by accident and then you help us to make the best of it, and that's the part we are supposed to have faith in.

Of course, that makes you like a clean-up hitter in the bottom of the ninth, but what the hell. Those guys are heroes, and a hero God who saves the day is a slightly more adrenalized action hero, though in the same comforting vein as a Santa God, who gives you your every desire.

I think about all this, God, because I have another notion that is coming clear to me, perhaps coming clear as I write to you. It's a thought that goes something like: "Do something yourself." Have the faith to look in the paper for a new apartment. Have the faith to look through the want ads and talk to people about new work. Have the faith to "do the footwork," as they say, and then maybe the God part—are you listening?—is helping somehow with that. Like maybe I throw the switch of willingness and you help me with the juice to carry through.

I could use a little juice to carry through right now. My life feels like a jigsaw puzzle that I dropped while carrying its thousand pieces from the kitchen table to the living room. Now it's all over the floor and I know it must fit back together somehow, but it's an awful lot of work and I've lost the box, so I don't even have a picture of what it is I am supposed to be making. Mount Fuji or a charging elephant—which is it?

Dear God,

You may know this already, but I've actually taken my life in my hands and hired a realtor to look for a new living space. Don't you like how trendy I've become? "Living space." It brings out a morbid humor. Is there such a thing as a "dying space"? That's how my own place feels.

The realtor says I will have "lots of lovely options." She says that a man of my means is in an enviable position. This probably means she's checked my credit and believes me that I can make a down payment. She's just full of cheery news. "I'm sure we'll find you something beautiful." Beautiful would be nice, but I'd settle for livable. When I found this place, it was the first one I'd seen that didn't feel like a mausoleum. Jolly old St. Nick, aren't I?

Dear God,

Not to put too fine a point on it—I cannot stand people who are constantly taking their emotional temperature—I feel a creeping sense of, alright, optimism. It has occurred to me that this could be an answered prayer. I have been griping and complaining in your direction, and perhaps you got so sick of it that you did something, or perhaps you were just the wailing wall I needed and I did something—I wailed on your shoulder.

Wasn't there once a prayer form called "lamentations"? Maybe I am just a modernist practitioner. Maybe griping at you instead of just playing emotional roulette in my head actually has given me some surcease.

You will notice—as I have—that I have not leapt to the conclusion that my improved mental condition is an answered prayer. Maybe it's a scary thought to me that you might actually be listening and moved to do something. Maybe I am a lot more comfortable with the idea of your absence than your presence. Maybe this is why so much of what could be construed as answered prayer is more often and more comfortably chalked up to coincidence. Maybe I just happened to cheer up—fat chance.

When I undertook writing to you, it was because the other options seemed like dead ends to me—more therapy, antidepressants, some good old-fashioned substance abuse, a meaningless fling, etc. You seemed to be the one alternative in which I didn't know the probable outcome.

I still don't, and this perky mood of mine pretty much proves it.

Dear God,

My sister is thinking of reconciling with her rat husband. I'm back on the horns of my dilemma. Should I tell her what a womanizing bastard I think he is, or should I just stay out of it? Actually, I can understand her urge to take him back. Being alone isn't easy, although I would say it's easier than being with someone who doesn't love you. My New Age friend, the one who thinks of you as an invisible playmate, also believes in what she calls "soul mates." My understanding is that a soul mate is the person you've been missing all your life, the one who mysteriously matches your every nook and cranny. What is that expression, "The rocks in my head fit the holes in his?" Maybe that's my sister's lot. Maybe the rat really is her soul mate. Maybe they could at least go to marriage counseling so that one or the other, the divorce or the marriage, would stick. I hear myself using terrible phrases such as, "I'm there for you," when I talk to my sister. I'm not there. Nobody really is. Friends can only do so much. At least I haven't told my sister to get a hobby. Are you telling her anything? Are you on speaking terms? I'm afraid to ask her.

Dear God,

So much for optimism. I'm depressed as hell about my sister.

Today's mood may be less pessimism than banked fury: Exactly how do you cope with free will? Do we always disappoint you, making less of ourselves than we could or should? Do we habitually fail to honor commitments, or is that just my dismal experience with people, and, on balance, do we do better than that? I'd like to think *yes*, but that leaves me feeling a little bit like a spiritual tar baby—collecting disappointment and resentment at every turn.

Dear Lord, how did it feel when Peter didn't know you—three times? I do not grapple well with betrayal. It can take me out for a decade or so at a whack—witness my lack of bounce-back following my relationship imploding. Did my beloved's new beloved have to be someone I knew? (Familiarity breeds *attempt?* Ha, ha.) Did my ego really need to be ground through such fine gears? Oh, I have experienced powerlessness in the face of free will. We cannot make people love us, and we cannot make people do as we wish. That being said, is one of your major functions to hand out the Kleenex?

Dear God,

Is the world so various because you knew we would always want more? Lately I do. I've got all kinds of inchoate cravings. I heard a pundit say that humans contain "a hole the size of God." Well, I can tell you it is not the size of a new leather sofa or a BMW or the great new stereo I got on sale. It is not even the size of a Significant Other—although a lot of my friends seem to think it might be, and they go through an astounding array of new SO's looking for one that makes them feel better, like a people-form Prozac. I could try smoking dope, but I didn't even like it as a kid, and the liquor ads with their sizzling glances and promises of nights of passion are just plain embarrassing.

I haven't asked you how you feel about true love. Do you suspect it's a marketing ploy? I don't like to think we have a one and only. It makes the odds of missing them too high. Have you heard the expression "God shot?" It means something good that happens against all odds. I could use a God shot, God.

Dear God,

The realtor has shown me fifteen "possibilities." I feel like I'm auditioning lives or monkeying with my destiny. How do you keep track of all of us? Do you know who lives in 6A, and do you notice when they move into a larger space in 4B? It's an awful lot to keep track of. Perhaps not for you. I worry about things like changing my address. Will my mail find me? Will some bill go unpaid? Will I miss an invitation to the party that would have changed my life, introducing me to my true love? On the other hand, maybe my true love will live across the hall, and I just need the courage to move so we can meet.

Dear God,

I am back to something I think you must be able
to identify with: My life would be fine if only *they*
would do what I want. We must drive you crazy!
"We" certainly drive me crazy. My boss is biting
people's heads off. My sister is still waffling about
her louse of a husband. Can it really be your will
for people to stay unhappily wed? I don't think so.
You can correct me on this, but that business about
"offering it up" to you must keep an awful lot of
people stuck—of their own free will—in misery instead of moving into lives and relationships in which
they could function better and perhaps do some
good. I know that when I offer something up, the
something I offer is usually my simmering resentment. That does not exactly make me feel clear and
expansive and generous about what I can give to
this world.

But back to this idea of free will. Yes, yes, I like having it—but do we have it? Do we shape our fates or simply live them out? Right now, for example, this misty misery I am stumbling through like a bad B movie fog—is this because I have strayed off the path? Is there a path? If I pray, will you show it to me? Or are there perhaps multiple paths, all fine with you, that we elect and select ourselves— but perhaps best with an assist from you?

Looking back, I can see that many no's where I felt impossibly thwarted actually worked out to be yesses in disguise. I think it's this way for a lot of things, a lot of people. One of my friends did not win the woman he wanted—she stayed with her boyfriend and just kept flirting with him. Well, he finally broke it off. She married the boyfriend—and then cheated on him as one might have suspected. My friend thinks he got off light. I do, too. Yet, when I get a no from you, I never think, *Ah, good, I'm getting off light again*. I think something more along the lines of, *Damn you, God! I wanted this!*

The want, of course, is self-will. Or my will. But don't your will and mine sometimes coincide? Can't they? Are they always at opposite ends of the table? A lot of religions seem to think so. I have even heard it from 12-steppers. "If you want something, you can be pretty sure it's not God's will for you." Says who?

Maybe all of this free-will-versus-God's-will brouhaha is really something we need to parse out a case at a time. Maybe it's not cause for conflict, just conversation. Maybe my having that thought is an answered prayer.

Is it?

Dear God,

It's a little situation at work. To be blunt: I'm right. I'm right. I know it. They will know it, but by then it will be too damn late. Why is it that people don't listen? Why is it that when you see something clearly and it's a good, helpful thing you're seeing, people let their little corporate egos get all riled up, as if because it's not their idea, they shouldn't support it? What happened to "we're all in this together"? Just a little cooperation and we would all be in a much better boat.

Is that sound your chuckling? It occurs to me that you may have these thoughts regarding warring nations—or even political parties. It must be uncomfortable—that's a polite word—to have all manner of carnage and genocide committed in your name. I imagine you are all too familiar with the thought, *Why can't they play team ball?*

Why can't they?

Dear God,

A few letters back, I dimly broached the idea that I had not broached the idea of a relationship. I think that was my roundabout way of hinting to you that, yes, all right, maybe I did want one after all, if only you would save me from getting creamed.

It's funny, but these few weeks of writing to you have helped me see that the root of the whole idea may have been as simple as: I'm lonely. Maybe I was lonely for you, God, but also maybe I was just plain lonely. I think that as we go on in life and our stories get longer, we tend to crave somebody who can help us make sense of the narrative, somebody who can witness the chapters as they unfold and maybe help us parse out what they mean. Back when we had villages instead of cities, we also had witnesses. The extended family included an extended view. "I knew you when you were a toddler" is not something you hear a lot if your career has taken you out of Des Moines and plunked you down in Midtown Manhattan. I think I miss having some elders. I think I miss having that kind of encouragement from someone a little farther down the trail. So maybe I have turned to you in these cobbled-together missives, hoping that you actually will be a little like Obi-Wan Kenobi and that you will put a celestial comforting arm around my shoulder and give me some sense that I am doing fine—or that I will be.

I am not sure where we came up with that phrase "significant other." What about "lover," "spouse," "partner," "friend"? What about "someone to watch over me"? Maybe the still, small voice could sound a little like Willie Nelson's?

I have noticed something funny about these prayers. I write them out and raise some issue, and then I notice a day or two later that there has been some shift. I don't get a major burning bush, but I do get a wisp of change like the trail of smoke in the autumn—faint but real. Oh, God, you subtle devil—whoops.

You know what I mean.

Dear God,

Here is a new and unpleasant thought: Maybe that chestnut, "God helps those who help themselves," is actually good advice. Take this wrinkle: I think a lot of boredom is actually depression and vice versa. I think a little action would clear up a lot of it, and I think most of us would rather blame you than get off our duffs.

I don't like my apartment, but I don't look harder for a new one because "there aren't any." How do I know that? Other people find them. I am tired of reading the same newspaper every day, no matter how lofty, but do I get a subscription to something a little off my beaten track? No. My hobbled computer skills keep me from exploring a lot of intellectual territory that might interest me, but I don't ante up the energy to look for a computer class. "I'm too tired."

Well, what I am really tired of is the fact that I am on my little treadmill, blaming it all on you. I can read the want ads; I can let my fingers do the walking. All I need is willingness. I can pray for willingness.

Oops.

Dear God,

This business of writing you prayers is hell on my self-pity. It seems to me that the more I broach things to you, the more you broach them back to me. For example, take yesterday's point about inertia: Today I opened one of the sidewalk boxes that hold those catalogues advertising adult courses. Yes, there was one on computers that is so close by, it almost meets in my building. At a convenient time. At a good price. And, of course, if I got computer literate I could look at housing on the Internet, which is the modern way to do it, I am told. God, I hate the modern way of doing things, don't you?

No, probably not. You probably really love invention—look at all that you yourself did. Just take dogs. Rottweilers. Spaniels. Westies. Boxers. Dachshunds. Great Danes. Golden retrievers. Scotties. German shepherds. You get my point—or I get yours. Maybe they used to call you the Creator for a reason. Maybe your creations used to be more in evidence when our own were more modest. Cities are perhaps more monuments to our ingenuity, while mountains and forests and meadows and wetlands and willow trees and finches and all that good stuff might make us think more of you—which is probably why New Yorkers love Central Park.

So, to circle back to how I write something to you and then you "right" my attitude, I see that these letters are a form of asking for clarity and help and that—whoops!—I am getting some. Yes, I can take a computer course. Yes, I can find better housing. No, my miserable life is not your fault, although it might be mine, and between the two of us we can actually change it, can't we?

Tomorrow, could we discuss synchronicity?

Dear God,

What is it that makes people want to point fingers and blame?

Did I hear you say, "Let them off the hook"?

I am distracted today. I want to point fingers and blame. I want to say, "If only they [would do what I want], then I . . ." The truth is that I want my life to change, but it's hard to put my shoulder to the wheel to do it. For one thing, I picture change in such wholesale, terrifying ways that I leap back from the cliff, yelping, "I can't do that!" meaning I can't move to France to get peace and quiet. (No, but I could unplug my phone.) Or about exercise: "I don't have time to train for a marathon!" No, but I could walk on a treadmill for fifteen or twenty minutes, or get off a stop early on the subway and walk a few blocks, or—here's a really terrible idea—put on some old Beatles or Motown and dance for ten minutes *in the privacy of my own home.*

I could do a lot of things—small things—that I don't do because I think in such grandiose terms that I scare myself out of doing anything. I think, *I should get a masters degree,* not, *I could take a piano lesson.* I think, *Jesus, Mary and Joseph! I need to get all new furniture!* not, *A little rug would help in front of the sink.* Not, *I could get a gizmo to hold all the shower stuff that keeps falling into the tub.*

The point is, I think I am catching on to the fact that if I keep focusing on how you—and all my global neighbors—are botching up the world, well, then I don't need to get a bookcase or fix the shower curtain, do I? If I am always focused on the Big Picture, I don't see the ways to husband my little part of it, do I?

Oh, you are sneaky, God. Or maybe you have mastered the art I am talking about. Maybe your eye is on the sparrow so you don't have to look at the big picture, either. Maybe one little bit, one short day at a time, this world is beautiful and doable after all.

Dear God,

I am exhausted. Do you know what that feels like? Do you actually feel or do you just have concepts? The concept here is "every bone aches and I am drained of all optimism." I am trying to avoid melo-drama, pathos, and the conviction that my life is sliding inexorably downhill, but it is astounding how lonely a little bit too much fatigue can make you. Or maybe a little too much loneliness makes you fatigued. I think it works both ways.

I haven't been writing to you for long, but I have been writing to you long enough for me to realize that I am being coy about the whole arena of personal relationships. I believe I told you that my friends are acceptable—a tepid word. I have no sig-nificant other at this time, as you well know. I may have one again—but I sometimes feel as though that would take a miracle, which reminds me that miracles are your line of work, not mine. Could you get to work?

I feel as though I am flopping in the self-transformation business, and so I had better turn it over to you, the actual transformation expert—or so I've been told. I figure if St. Paul could have a spiritual awakening—even if it did take getting blasted off his horse to do it—maybe I can have one, too. I don't need a burning bush. I don't need the Virgin of Guadalupe to appear and fill my over-coat with roses. What I do need is a sense of meaning that goes beyond manners and convention and a job well done. I need something that feels actually nutritious to what I hesitatingly call my soul. In other words, I am conscious that some deeper part of myself is starving despite my friends, my work, my sundry personal and professional ties. My heart is both restless and exhausted. I want to hear some higher harmonic than the nightly news, but I am not sure how to listen for it.

Sometimes, walking home from work, I think

I catch it. Maybe it's just a trick of the light, but sometimes, even though I am tired and the day has been long, I realize that the sea of human faces moving toward me is very beautiful and that we are all in this somehow together and that it is fine. I love that feeling. I wish I could carry it with me more often, but it seems to come on a whim and vanish the same way that amazing cobalt blue you see at evening's end is there just for a minute and then gone.

God, could you send me a sense of meaning more often? If you told me where the mailbox was, I'd walk there to get it.

Dear God,

I am going to bring this up: Alone, I am just a hair less lonely.

I think it's your doing. Alright, maybe it's a little bit mine, too. I am not so much concerned with my inner movie since I have begun talking with you about it. I am a little more in the world. Maybe an inch more. I am like one of those soft-shell crabs without its shell—skittering out, trying a sandy toe's worth of new behavior and then trying to race back into his old shell, which doesn't fit anymore.

I am mad because it doesn't fit. I hate—let's say *hate*—the process of change. So I don't. And then I hate being stuck.

I think I am a little bit angry. OK, I think I am more than a little bit angry. Angry at myself. I think I have pretty thoroughly and consistently sold myself short. OK, I know I have.

I try to be fair. I try to turn the other cheek. I try to think good thoughts about people—but what it boils down to is denial. I have some people in my life who refuse to take the actions necessary to stand on their own two feet. So they stand on mine. And I let them. Is it any wonder I feel footsore? And have I added exhausted? What's the difference between helping and enabling? You should know.

I want a different kind of person in my life, but if they came to the door, I'd think they were the bogeyman or had the wrong address. They would, too, once they got a good look at my anger and self-pity.

Did I just hear you say I should call those things "exhaustion"? Are you Mary Poppins?

Dear God,

The gloves are off. No more nice-guy prayers. I hate my life. I hate knowing—thanks to you—that I can't blame it on you. I hate blaming it on me. It makes me *nuts.*

I'll line up the usual complaints: overworked, overtired, under-supported, undercooked—the last refers to what was supposed to have been a roast-chicken meal with mashed potatoes and savory gravy that I tried to eat at a diner on the way home from work. Do I need to add that I was out past my curfew and not getting overtime?

Did you just say, "Who asked you to?"

If I don't have to live this way to please you, then whose rotten idea is this? I thought martyrdom and self-effacement were your favorites? Your representatives are certainly a thin-lipped lot. They don't exactly exude the impression that frivolity and delight are God's will.

Daisies. Aardvarks. Puffer fish. Zebras. Giraffes. Mississippi mud pie. Espresso. New York street pizza. Calla lillies. Willow trees. Alright, I get the point. Life is not living hell—just my version of it. The bargain condo I hate. The sensible car that feels like driving a shoe. The great-benefits job that bores me out of my mind. Ten—OK, twenty—pounds that nibble at my conscience the way I've been known to nibble at Milano cookies.

I am tired of being sensible and coloring between the lines. I am tired of telling myself that this is your will for me. You certainly didn't do it yourself now, did you? And aren't fools and madmen actually among your favorites? Jesus was a hothead, mouthing off at the establishment, tossing the moneychangers out of the temple. And Buddha—naked as a jaybird, or nearly—sitting under a tree for ten years, waiting for enlightenment to fall and hit him on the head like Newton's apple.

Mother Teresa with those bright little beady eyes like some kind of spiritual squirrel. She wasn't exactly a model of decorum. So why should I be?

I want to study watercolor. I don't know why. I have always wanted a bomber jacket like the one Spencer Tracy wore in *A Guy Named Joe*. And, between you and me, I would like to tell my boss that he bores me to death, lacks vision, is a tightwad, and that his current course of "planning" looks like he's driving under the influence.

Maybe I'll indulge in all of the above. *That* would be a miracle.

Dear God,

What would it be like to believe in you? To feel safe?

If I believed in past lives—which I don't; this one is enough—I would say that I must have seen and lived through terrible things. A pogrom? A famine? The lopping off of limbs for stealing bread?

I have an implacable faith in catastrophe. I inwardly cry, "The sky is falling," 98 percent of the time. I exhaust myself, and I guess I exhaust myself because I do not believe in you—not a benevolent you. I act like nothing will turn out right without my worrying. It's like I think if I worry about something, I am paying you off by misery, so maybe something can work out right. I assume the worst— not about people, necessarily, but maybe about you. Or maybe about me. I am convinced of my own incompetence or maybe unlovability. I expect a pie in the face. When it comes, it's a relief. Trouble I can deal with. Imagined trouble is what I undergo.

All this makes me unnecessarily bitter. I soldier through, when a good laugh is what I really need. But I get much too serious and apocalyptic for mere laughter. I brood. I make drama. I do this because I do not know how to make whoopee. (Does that always, only, mean sex?)

I am sick of being depressive. I am sick of being worried. I also think the phrase "worried sick" may be quite accurate. My worry wears me down. It occurs to me Job may have been a whiner. Have you heard the joke about you and Job?

JOB: Why me, God?

GOD: I don't know, Job, you just kind of piss me off.

Dear God,

I seem to have some insomnia going. I am tired of it (ha, ha). I rotated all night, again, on the spit of my imaginings—all bad. I never imagine Happy Endings. I never bask in my successes or the feeling of who loves me—and some people really may.

My glass is always half empty. It is always going to be a long trek through the desert. My rations never last long enough, etc. Talking to you, I think even Jesus despaired, "Father, Father, why have you forsaken me?" I have heard that anguish explained away as, "He really meant . . ." I think he really meant exactly what he said. I think even God—if Jesus was God—felt that God, if there is one at all, *had* forsaken him. (It's easy to see how he leapt to that conclusion, hanging on a cross.)

Well, I leap to that conclusion myself—every

time I feel like I am hanging on a cross. Every time, especially when I get that little glimmering that I am the one who climbed up there.

I am the one who overworks. I am the one who chooses thankless friends. I am the one who clings to difficult jobs and personal situations. I just blame it on you and then wonder why you have abandoned me. I think, perhaps, I have abandoned me. And if the still, small voice that they talk about does mean God lives within us, as they say, then I have abandoned both of us.

There's a thought.

Maybe you could teach me how to be kinder. Maybe you could help me feel less scared. Worry is fear, isn't it? It is certainly a refusal to have faith. I have heard the saying, "Faith without works is dead." And I have gotten worked up instead of letting you help me work it out—whatever "it" is.

"Move out on faith," the preachers say. Am I just stubborn? Every time I try, good things happen. And, oh, yes, I need good things. I just won't reach for them, or maybe I'd ask you to send me a ladder. No, instead I obsess about how good things are beyond my reach. I think I took the part about getting slapped for reaching for the apple a little too seriously.

Dear God,

All the great spiritual traditions talk about surrender. I am pretty sure that if I surrendered to you, to believing in you, I'd end up in a POW camp somewhere I hated. Isn't that what surrender means?

I am not sure when I decided to do without you. I think I got so fed up with religion—and my abuse of it, I might add, aided and abetted by a few spiritual Nazis who helped me feel *really* bad about myself—that I took religion to be you. Or at least your idea.

Some people seem to be gleeful sinners. Not I. And the faith (well, they do call it that) that I grew up with fostered what I now see as a morbid, even neurotic sense of self-loathing grounded in Original Sin and the many further sins, especially those around impure thoughts and deeds. Try not to think about sex when you are an adolescent. Try not to touch him, her, or *it*. That. Down there. God's big mistake. Oops. Sexuality. Well, it certainly felt like my mistake.

I did not cut a wide swathe, but cutting one at all cut me to ribbons. And so I rationally, or irrationally, as it now seems, decided to fire God based on his evident henchman, Religion. Why I singled that out as your creation and skipped things such as sea anemones and dandelion puffs is beyond me.

And now that I have committed so many—and so few—of the things Catholics call "mortal" sins, I feel like there's no going back but also no going forward without you or without Something. And I suspect that something is you, in some form.

If I surrendered to the idea that I might need you, need some kind of relationship to you, would you march me into a wire enmeshment, otherwise known as a church? Would you help me at least get

over my idea that God is for the intellectually im-
paired? If I'm so smart, how did I come up with that
dumb idea? Do I know how to make even a simple
paramecium?

Dear God,

My head hurts. My back has a peculiar knot in it. My feet have some funny soreness. My eyes are bothering me—somehow I thought I would be immune to a vision shift—and I notice that the heat in my house isn't warm enough, except when it's much too warm.

That's my little litany of woes. I am tired of thinking about me, and I bet you are, too. Or maybe thinking about all of us takes your mind off you and off the question, the *big question*: Did I screw this up when I gave them free will?

I am tinkering with an idea that may have come from you. Or maybe it came from me, and that is you moving through me, as the mystics say. "Not I but the Father doeth the work." OK, enough vamping. Here's the thought: Maybe there isn't such separation between You Up There and Us

Down Here. Maybe looking for you out there or up there has kept me from finding you inside. The last place I would ever look is in me.

I also think it's not just in me. It's in us. I think reaching out to someone else allows me to feel some current. Maybe when they reach back and we feel them, that is feeling you, or you in them.

Let me tell you what happened. I was in the part of my head I call "Whirry" (Worry). It's the part where my mind speeds up and shows me Scary Movies Non Stop and I get the Doomsday Voice-Over. Instead of just listening to it, watching the movie, and believing it was likely, I tried focusing on something. Facts. One fact. Then another. Then another. When I did that, I felt a solution pop up like toast. "Try this." I am going to suggest to my sister that she find a good therapist.

Facts: I feel better since writing you this letter. My head hurts less. I see I can just go get under the covers. Good night.

Dear God,

Or maybe I should say, "Oh dear, God!"

I seem to be having a disconcerting number of answered prayers, what I might have previously— and still would like to—dismiss as coincidence, luck, or "synchronicity," that term of Jung's for when something clear in the inner world is met with un- canny accuracy by something in the outer world.

All my griping to you has led me to the clear realization that I can act on my own behalf in small ways without burning my house down and that you will meet and support my actions with actions of your own. (I did not write that sentence; I could not have. It sounds like "faith.") What I see is that Some- thing Weird—and, alright, good—is going on. I bought a little rug for near the sink and a gizmo to hold my shower stuff. I am even enjoying my real estate outings. There is a dance that "we" seem to be doing. I have to tell you, it makes a lot of scripture seem a little more plausible: "Knock and it shall be opened to you"; "Ask and you shall receive."

As you may have gathered, I am not a big truster. But it has occurred to me that trust might be learned and that I can open my mind enough to try a little experimentation. I guess by writing these letters, I am doing that. I don't think of them as prayers exactly, but they may be. I suppose they are.

Dear God,

I always thought prayer had to be rigid, and it didn't seem to match my spiritual attitude. I had a lot of gripes and grievances, so I wasn't too thrilled with prayers like "Our Father." Not all of us have had the greatest fathers. (You may have noticed that.) Hey, I just realized that maybe that prayer was intended to mean you could step in where they botched it! See what I mean about my getting new ideas? But back to the prayer business. I did not think it could be casual. I thought it had to be formal, and I thought it had to be on bended knees and that it really boiled down to either "help me" or "OK, OK, what the hell do you want me to do?" This idea of a conversation, a gentle nudge and not a shove—that's all new and it's all pretty radical for me.

Old hat to you, I suppose. What is it, "Pray unceasingly?" They should have said "talk" or "chat" or something user-friendly. (My opinion.)

Dear God,

Please help me—it seems I do need your help. Let me rephrase it. "Dear God, God help me!" (That feels a little less like real prayer.)

I have progressed from depression and a certain caged complacency to what might be called stark terror. My life is changing. I want it to change. But I want it to change without changing, if you know what I mean—which you'd better or I am in real trouble.

A letter at a time—alright, a prayer at a time—I have been trying to nudge open the door to my mind, although you might call it my soul. Perhaps it is my soul. My mind has run things for such a long time and has run me straight into the ground, if you want to know the truth. I am now at my wit's end, which might be a good thing. It might be surrender, as the spiritual people call it—and maybe surrendering to a need for spiritual help is less like losing the war than admitting the obvious and maybe even winning the war.

You know the war I am talking about—the war between feeling the world to be one thing and spirit another; the body is one thing and spirit is another. I am toying with the idea—which may have come from you, or even from you in me—that the world, the body, and the spirit are all intermingled and interconnected. That we are all one, as I have heard that the mystics say. Well, I am not a mystic. Or, if I am, maybe I am a very ordinary, everyday mystic, and maybe we all are. Maybe all of us can reach you and reach these thoughts just by trying a little. I am trying a little and—

And all hell has broken loose!

My slightly bitter and a little bit smug resignation has now been replaced with a sickening free fall, occasionally giddy but occasionally a plummet with the sure knowledge that I have no parachute. Are you—or a belief in you—supposed to be a safety net? You damn well better be.

I have moved out on faith, just as advised, and you know what? It feels a hell of a lot like thin ice— maybe even like I am skidding across, about to fall into the black and frigid depths.

But maybe not.

Is thinking *maybe not* about disaster some amoeboid form of faith?

Dear God,

They say confession is good for the soul. Are "they" some kind of spiritual voyeurs? These letters, I suppose, are a form of confession to you. How do you feel about all my caviling and reservations? Do you ever want to snap, "Trust me, goddamn it! I made the entire universe!"

Maybe you have infinite patience. Maybe that's what the vast swathe of stars means—not numbing indifference at the sheer numbers, but unimaginable care counting every atom, every particle speeding through space.

What if you do care? What if we are safe in the long run? The very long run, that is. A few wars, a few zillion deaths, but all of it tending on some huge imponderable scale toward the good?

Before we get to that big unimaginable good, I need help with the job situation, with finding some new dishes, and with a non-chintzy bookcase that doesn't cost more than the beater I drove in high school. When they talk about the rising cost of living, do you think it is just that as we age we notice the supposed cost of things and that when we are young we have the deep pockets of youthful optimism?

I am wondering if I believed more in you and in me as a youngster and then lost faith in both of us as the world—meaning religions and institutions and bosses and all manners of supposed authority—began telling me who each of us was. We both got small somehow.

Talking to you on the page, we both seem to be getting a little bigger and perhaps a little more likable—don't we?

Dear God,

I used to think it was crazy to believe in you. Look
at the Holocaust! Look at those children with legs
and arms like sticks and those huge, gentle eyes!
How could there be a God who would allow that?

I am pretty sure "we" are who allowed that. I
am pretty sure that it is much crazier to blame the
big picture on you than it might be to try being nice
to someone. In a small way. The milk of human kind-
ness. That's divine. And maybe that is also how we
contact you most directly. In other words, instead
of making you an abstract and blamable something,
maybe you are more concrete, more embodied, more
right here, and a belief in creation itself is really a
belief in a creator—we just don't admit it or see it
that way very much.

Or maybe people wiser than I do. But I am a
beginner at this God stuff and am probably tell-

ing you a story you have heard many, many times before.

My ego would normally object to that idea. It would want to be "special." It's not doing that about this, though. It is finding a certain relief in the idea of shared humanity. It is finding a creature comfort in the thought that we are all in this together, instead of "them" versus me or my other antiquated stance: me versus you. Maybe it was me versus me all along. Maybe in fighting my need for there to be a you, I was ignoring a biggish part of me—the part of me that is you, or at least connected to you.

I am not a mystic, or are we all?

Dear God,

It occurred to me this morning that I could try taking a cue from your "seasons" concept. (Now this may seem obvious to you, but to me it was something of a revelation.)

I think I could learn a little patience with myself if I took a view of myself that included concepts like dormancy (instead of laziness), seed planting (instead of just scattered), gestation (instead of do-something-right-this-second). Maybe I could learn a little to trust your timing and my timing. In short, maybe I could learn to do "process."

As I have said, I hate change. To me, it has always seemed to be so violent. Yet, change is what I am hoping for. "Violent" may seem like a dramatic word to you for something as simple as a job change. Or a relationship ending. But in my life, these have been the forest fires, the earthquakes, the tidal waves. However, I think that if I build bridges as well as burn them, change could be less violent.

Looking at the "seasons" concept again, I do see that new growth has come from the burnings, new stability and forms have come from rebuilding after my heart quakes, and that even with the terrible tidal waves, I have found myself to be, frankly, one hell of a swimmer. (Floating spars you've sent along have helped, too.)

Dear God! Optimism!

Dear God,

I want to talk with you a little more about this business of change. It is clear to me that instead of having compassion for myself (A) or trust in you (B), what I normally have is something like stark terror—and a lot of judgment about that.

I think that I need to learn a few different modalities of change: gradual and grounded like a seed growing and, too, when it is time to leap lest I be left hanging over a chasm clutching frantically to either side. In other words, I may need to listen to guidance about when to edge forward and when to leap forward. What clearly does not serve me is trying to meet every situation with an obdurate set mode. Maybe you could set the tempo? I'd listen.

Back to you and the seasons: Could I learn to be more attuned to life's different weathers? To know when it is a sunny day, a windy day, a terrible storm, just threatening, hot, cold, temperate? I think what I am asking is to become less defended and more able to dance with life's rhythms instead of trying to make life march to mine. In other words, maybe I don't need to carry an umbrella every day and then complain about how the sun is never out.

I think I am edging toward a very foreign idea: that you may care about, and even take care of, me.

Dear God,

I know you are big on "the lilies of the field." I know that "on the seventh day" you rested. Well, I am not a lily of the field and on the seventh day I am usually still playing catch-up ball. I thought this made me virtuous, the work ethic and all that. Or maybe it's just drabs of leftover Calvinism. Now I am wondering if all my work doesn't render me an ingrate.

It has occurred to me: Maybe I am supposed to enjoy being here. When I slow down, even for a minute, I do enjoy it. Last night the sunset was one of those acrylic paint-kit numbers—impossibly pink and neon, struck through with a real gold and ruby red. OK, so it's the smog or something. I loved it. I actually stopped and looked at it and loved it.

This is a new wrinkle for me. Taking time to stop, I mean.

I have been taking the time to pet strange dogs, to say a few cheery words at the checkout counter. I have started to feel a little like Jimmy Stewart in *It's a Wonderful Life*. Maybe that's because I have stopped playing *It's a Horrible Life* as the movie in my head.

I have begun to lighten up. I have noticed that life's comedy is as prevalent as life's tragedy—not, perhaps, on CNN, but on the street.

There is a beggar—I guess the politically correct term is "homeless person"—who I regularly hand a dollar to. I have taken the unusual step of asking his name and using it. Not that this makes me wonderful, but it does make him a little more real. I think when I hurry along, rabid, rapid and miserable, it keeps things blurred and a little numbed. Pain is a dull ache, and joy? That's not something I could feel much of.

Today, passing a window with a full load of flowers, I watched an orange cat carefully disemboweling a splendid floret of geranium. I felt joy.

Dear God,

Dawn was particularly nice—not that I wanted to see it. It was pink and glowed like the inside of a conch shell does when you hold it to the light— nice work.

Meanwhile, I am a piece of work. I was up viewing, if not enjoying, your sunrise because I was wild with anxiety. "Wild with anxiety" is a specialty of mine. It has to do with my wanting a change, getting it, and then absolutely panicking that I have made a mistake.

In my version of events, spiritual help is like CPR—good in an emergency, but not something you ask for all the time. It's like I am afraid of cry- ing wolf and so I am learning—did you notice that? I am learning to ask for help with biggish things, but I consider asking for help with smallish things to be beneath your dignity and mine, even if the smallish things are what are driving me crazy. And they are.

A smallish thing? OK, yesterday I was snappish. I could see it on the face of the receptionist I was talking to. A sort of almost imperceptible eyebrow to the hairline, meaning, "Another one of those . . ."

I don't want to be another one of "those." And I don't want to treat people like they are, either. I want to be something more or better than grumpy, stiff, irate, harried, worried, frantic, panicked, barely keeping a lid on it.

So maybe I better start asking for help—or at least companionship during the small things.

Don't you think that it's the long line at the bank, the remarkably long line at the post office, the way it takes forever at the drug store, and the way those checkout clerks are all set on Very Slow that make us want to snap each other's heads off? I mean, I don't want to think it's just me. I don't want to think I am a Type A—as in you know what.

So could you help me find vacuum bags? I am taping the one I've got because nobody has my exact nine number one. And I've got dust. Should I mention that until I get a new place, I've been taking much better care of the one I've got?

Dear God,

You may remember that I asked you if we are intended to stay in rotten situations and offer it up? I no sooner broached the question than a door opened. I may have a line on another—and perhaps better—job. I hope so. I *really* hope so.

I have been working meanwhile on remaining civil in the one I have got. Don't snap at the receptionist. Don't fire off memos—or glances—that communicate, "Everything you are doing and everything about you is wrong."

Instead, buy an African violet for the receptionist. Bring in extra little cartons of milk for the staff refrigerator instead of just wondering why it disappears and you are stuck with that lousy, clumpy creamer.

I almost think I can hear you laughing about

all this, like maybe I am catching on. Am I catching on?

I talked with my sister with the louse husband. She said I sounded different. I told her it might be very nice to have a little kitten or something to give her some love.

Maybe I should get a kitten.

Dear God,

How do you do it? (And please don't say, "I'm God and you're not.")

Today, I wish I were. When I say, "How do you do it?" I mean, "How do you listen to heartbreak or see something moving toward it, like a boat over the falls, and not reach down and just save the day?" I wish I could save the day for my sister right now.

It goes like this: Her husband is a phony, and she can sense it but not face it. I can see it, but what can I say? "There's something really fishy in the character of the main person in your life"? I think he's got another woman, or several. He certainly wishes he did. And if wishes were horses, that guy would have a herd. I hate to see her thinking all the time, *What am I doing wrong? What's wrong with me?* I want her to figure this out, but I also know the pain that will be there when she does. And I think a handy car wreck—your department—wouldn't work either, because then she'd never know what a rat he was and would probably go to her grave thinking it was her. What the hell do you do, God?

You probably do things like I try to—urge her to build on what she can to feel better about herself. Take a class maybe? Try a hobby? See more of her friends? There is still something rotten in Denmark and that stuff is the window dressing that works to a point, but not if your house is burning down. So I think I smell smoke. Do you?

Dear God,

Do you come to us as hunches? Is the still, small voice what gets us into the right stores on sale days?

I have noticed that if I get clear about wanting something, you—or something—seem to work out a way to help me have it. That is, if I nudge the door open the tiniest inch toward getting things in motion—I make one phone call—and then I run into several pretty spooky coincidences. Are you the spooky coincidence part?

Maybe so, eh?

I am, as you know, not so fond of the job situation. I feel like it's a sort of low-grade infection. No matter what I do, I can't quite shake the sickish feeling that I've got about the place. I've tried mentioning this a little to my colleagues, and they act as if I'm nuts. I feel like either I am or they are really in denial. I am beginning to feel like that guy from *Invasion of the Body Snatchers* who noticed that maybe people weren't quite acting real. Either I really need a new job or I really need a lobotomy. Maybe my lead will pan out. Alternatively, maybe this place will turn around. Am I starting to believe in miracles?

I am wondering if my trying to talk with you hasn't caused some of this. Maybe trying to contact God makes you feel a little less embedded in life as it seems to be and a little more open to life as it could be. And that, damn it, means that you notice things that aren't in line with your ethics, which you suddenly find that you've actually got!

It occurs to me that the word "conscience" means "with knowing." Maybe we get our "knowing" from trying to talk with you. In any case, my knowing is now on red alert and I think my company—and some of the company I keep, for that matter—is a little too sleazy, maybe a little too profit-oriented instead of product-oriented, and maybe it all feels second-rate and my working there makes me feel that way, too.

Am I becoming grandiose? Or more honest? What the hell am I supposed to do? All right. I *am* asking.

Dear God,

I wonder what it would be like if that were more like a term of affection and less like a formal salutation.

"Dear" God. Or even, "God, dear . . ."

I know that mystics—Christian and otherwise—talk about God as the "beloved." Well, that's always struck me as a little carnal and tacky. I knew a girl once—a rather overheated girl—who told me she always kissed the crucifix on the lips. I felt like saying, "Jesus Christ! Get a grip!"

Maybe she did have a grip. Maybe she could see what there was to love, even if in a rather too human way. I, on the other hand—or all six hands like those dancing Balinese statues—could never see the positive. I was all about what was wrong with you, not what you might have done right—mountains, fir trees, hawks, and those funny little pale pinky-white early spring flowers I used to pick as a kid. Of course, there's more right than just those things, but my point is that you would think I might love you for some of that stuff instead of acting like all of the beauty were some random accident—while all non-beauty was your fault. I've had this thought before, but not so forcefully. Am I beginning to be on your side? Am I beginning to see your point of view?

In short, I have concluded that I have been a thankless ingrate. A lot of what I thought of as my compassion—all those suffering children, how can there be a God?—may have actually been a thinly veiled snobbery. If I'd been God, I'd have done it so much better. . . . As if you hadn't matched the plaids or something.

So, "dear" God, I want to say that I like my crotchety little neighbor lady who snoops on everyone and talks my ear off. I never thought I liked her, but I have noticed lately that I actually seem to. Her gossip seems more like human interest and less like static than it used to. Am I getting less busy and important? Is she getting more interesting? I have always wondered about the thing that spiritual people say about how you love us all equally. How could you? That is superhuman.

Which you are.

Dear God,

I have concluded that I have been pretty cranky and bitter and lonely. (I do not hear a gasp of surprise.) I thought I was fashionably alienated and experiencing something dignified like nihilism or existentialism. Now I think maybe I was just sulking because things had not worked out as I thought they should, and I had only you to blame. (The alternative was blaming me, you see, although some people settle for blaming their parents.)

I have come to the conclusion that maybe I am stubborn. Or willful. Or both. Like my mother always said, I would get my heart set on something or somebody and then if I didn't get it— "That Teddy, Santa"—I would sulk, but in a well-disguised and dignified fashion, I think.

Modern sulking like mine is called "disillusionment" or "disenchantment." It is not called "I'll

take my marbles and go home, you fat bastard God."
But, in effect, that's what I did.

OK, I will not admire your wonderful rose
with the racy, red edging. I will not stop to pet that
cat. I will *not* call Aunt Bernice, even if I do remember it's her birthday. What I will do instead is think
a little bit more about me. . . .

Well, that diversion has paled, let me tell you.
Do you know the St. Francis prayer? Of course you
do. It's the one that goes, "Lord, make me an in-
strument of your peace. . . ." It's about being what
the Bible calls a "hollow reed" for the breath of God
to move through. Well, the idea isn't as appalling as
it used to be. I may like self-forgetting. It's a relief.

Dear God,

I am writing you these prayers, seeking to establish contact, and it turns out contact may be as simple as flicking a light switch. You do have to do it, but it's not so hard. I am toying with the idea that perhaps you are not so anthropomorphic and are maybe a little more like a form of spiritual electricity. As I suspected, my prayer is flicking the switch.

Of course, I could go on here about some saints getting fried from trying to run too much voltage without being properly grounded, but the point is that my perception has changed so that our difficulties seem to spring less from your erraticism and undependability and more from my own.

What a concept.

Dear God,

If you are a form of spiritual electricity, does that make you dangerous? Will I get electrocuted if I approach you the wrong way? Or are you more of a service like heat and light? It seems to me I am creeping around the idea of my having some kind of responsibility here as well. It might be partnering more than parenting you're after.

Maybe the people who want a mommy-daddy god don't want to grow up. Maybe the people who want God as Spiritual Law are a little numb to being hugged and made to feel cozy. Maybe to some people law is cozy, or at least safe. Maybe we get the experience of you that we can metabolize. For some people, you are in a snowflake or the tracery of Jack Frost on a windowpane. For others, you are the cathedral at Chartres and for others you are pure mathematics. I am not sure what you are to me, but

I am pretty sure that to you I am an awkward adolescent engaging in a dance that is old to you and new to me: getting to know you, getting to know all about you—or at least a lot more about me.

I see that my chronic avoidance and mistrust of you may have been a lot more rooted in my hiding out than your hiding out. You weren't the absentee landlord. I was the tenant who traveled all the time, lived in roadside hotels, and numbed out on cable (feeling vaguely superior to those using the Shopping Channel). The point is that I was in a world of my own instead of the glorious one that you had devised.

Oh, dear. It seems to me I may be covertly trying to cozy up to you. What has happened to my well-honed cynicism? Who am I without my intellectual defenses?

Dear God,

Alright. I have opened up the door. I have not seen a burning bush, but maybe I have put out the lit cigarette of cynicism smoldering in the sofa of my consciousness. And maybe I have seen the flicker of something higher and brighter—a little like a firefly: now you see it, now you don't. That's faith, I suppose, some tiny start on it.

More than a sense of anything massive and solid, I feel more like those first notes of a symphony about spring. I hear the birdsong of the flute. I sense change is afoot, and the huge orchestral swelling of a life made anew will come later. Today it's just the hyacinth bud pushing its nub of green upward through the cold earth. That's enough. There will be spring. There is spring if I don't get greedy and demand a whole riot of flowers all at once.

A lot of the changes you have wrought are so

small they are like that first faint greening on the trees—almost a vapor of green, a vapor of change and hope.

I have been granted patience—did I ask for that?—with my sister as she walked through this endless season of losing the house and doubting that she should get divorced at all. I have listened to the recitations of his faux virtues while she has grappled to admit his flaws and the fact that, anyhow, he has left.

I have been granted the courage to change. I might have asked for this, but like bringing home a puppy and later finding out it's a baby mastiff, it's more than I bargained for. I am changing—perhaps jobs, definitely the rules of the road in friendships, the arrangement of odds and bits in my medicine cabinet, how I deal with criticism at work. I seem to be becoming more outspoken, not in an aggressive way but in a more matter-of-fact way. I think this means I am a little more self-accepting, for example, I think now that I may have a right to my opinions and choices—reaching toward God has made me more me and not less me. I was always afraid you would erase me. Instead, you are helping me to sketch me in.

Dear God,

The realtor found me a place. It is spacious and sunny, with French windows and a tiny balcony. It's much nicer than where I am now—so nice, it seems like a miracle. The kitchen is big enough to cook in, the bathroom has a Jacuzzi jet, which seems a little bit too hip to me, but the living room has old-fashioned moldings, and the place feels solid. All in all, I'm in luck. Did I just hear you say, "Luck has nothing to do with it"? Should I take my lovely new space to be an answered prayer? If so, thank you and good work.

Dear God,

I bought a houseplant. Nothing spectacular, just a geranium, which I hear is hard to kill. It occurred to me that it would be healthy to have another living thing in my care. I confess I worry about it, whether there's enough sunlight until I get to the new place. How much water is the right amount, really? I read somewhere that we share musical tastes. Plants hate rock 'n' roll. They like Indian music and classical. I've taken to leaving my radio on classical when I go to work. Do plants' tastes reflect yours? Watch out for my geranium.

Dear God,

I have heard the phrase that faith should be "worn like a loose garment"—not a hair shirt—and I had this thought: I recently saw a photograph of some monks in a kitchen, baking, I think, Christmas fruitcakes. Those monks were all dressed exactly the same, in some ancient medieval sack knotted in at the waist; a glorified gunny sack, and each monk's face shone with an individual brightness and clarity as he went about his version of God's will: Get that loaf in the oven.

Maybe I am your loaf, God, and a little less half-baked than I was before trying to meet you. Maybe, like one of those monks, I am a little brighter as I go about the simple things.

About the Author

◆

Julia Cameron has been an active artist for more than thirty years. She is the author of eighteen books, fiction and nonfiction, including *The Artist's Way*, *Walking in This World*, *The Vein of Gold*, and *The Right to Write*, her bestselling works on the creative process. A novelist, playwright, songwriter, and poet, she has multiple credits in theater, film, and television. Cameron divides her time between Manhattan and the high desert of New Mexico.

To order call 1-800-788-6262 or send your order to:
Penguin Putnam Inc.
P.O. Box 12289 Dept. B
Newark, NJ 07101-5289

Walking in This World	1-58542-183-9 hardcover	$24.95
The Artist's Way Tenth Anniversary Gift Edition	1-58542-147-2 hardcover	$40.00
The Artist's Way Audio	0-87477-852-2	$18.95
The Right to Write	0-58542-009-3 paper	$12.95
	0-87447-937-6 hardcover	$19.95
The Vein of Gold	0-87477-879-4 paper	$15.95
	0-87477-836-0 hardcover	$23.95
God Is No Laughing Matter	1-58542-128-6 paper	$13.95
	1-58542-065-4 hardcover	$19.95
The Artist's Date Book	0-87477-653-8	$14.95
The Artist's Way Morning Pages Journal	0-87477-886-7 paper	$14.95
Heart Steps	0-87477-899-9 paper	$9.95
	0-87477-901-4 audio	$10.95
Blessings	0-87477-906-5 paper	$9.95
	0-87477-907-3 audio	$11.95
Transitions	0-87477-995-2 paper	$9.95
	0-87477-996-0 audio	$11.95
Inspirations: Meditations from The Artist's Way	1-58542-102-2 paper	$6.95
The Writer's Life: Insights from The Right to Write	1-58542-103-0 paper	$6.95
Supplies: A Pilot's Manual for Creative Flight	1-58542-066-2 paper	$14.95
God Is Dog Spelled Backwards	1-58542-062-x paper	$9.95